Food for Thought

The Anointing of Discipline

I0162136

C V Lewis

YANA Ministries

YANA Ministries
He Answers

Publisher Yana Ministries
Year 2016

First Printing: 2016

ISBN 978-0-9935986-0-9
978-0-9935986-1-6

YANA Ministries
He Answers

Published by YANA Ministries
SE6, London, England
United Kingdom
www.yanaministries.wix.com/yana

Dedication

To my lovely husband and children.

For encouraging me and believing in me to accomplish greater dreams than I have ever dreamt.

Thank you. Without your support and patience, I would have never achieved my dream in writing and completing this book.

Contents

Acknowledgements...ix

Preface...xi

Introduction 1

Chapter 1: What is it all about...3

Chapter 2: The Power of Food..15

Chapter 3: Addictions 29

Chapter 4: Exercise...37

Chapter 5: Inner Desires...41

Chapter 6: Legalism vs Grace 53

Chapter 7: Freedom by the Word.....................................61

Notes...65

References 67

Acknowledgements

I would like to thank my family, without whose help this book would never have been completed.

Thank you for your patience and guidance, your use of the editor's red pen and humour to keep me focused through it all.

I would like to thank John Bevere for his inspiring messages and books I have been privileged to read. His testimony of the first book he ever wrote has been a focus keeping me moving forward.

I would like to thank Dr Myles Munroe who during his time of Ministry encouraged thousands not to take our talents and dreams to the cemetery. Who inspired many that we all have a purpose.

Preface

For years I had been in bondage to food, which started a few years before the birth of my third child. I started monitoring my food.

I became fearful to be free and eat certain foods, in fear I would gain more weight. I started to use exercise which I loved so much in the past, as a tool to burn off the fat which I gained through eating the wrong food.

For years I enjoyed buffets and would then retreat to eater's remorse the next day. Up and down I went emotionally, physically and spiritually until I realized the right way to deal with all areas of my life concerning food was spiritually first.

I started to search the scriptures and started to see victory as I applied it to my life.

I felt inspired to write this book as I saw the victory my testimony was bringing into the lives of those I shared the Word of God of with.

I also saw the same struggles I was having, repeated again and again in the lives of those around me and hoped to bring victory to them too.

Introduction

Food for thought has been written for those who have a bad relationship with food and for those who have a fairly good relationship, but would like it to be better. I am not just speaking to those who are over or underweight due to food, but even those that are at the right weight but heavily controlled by their desires and thoughts towards foods.

Let me ask you a question, could you walk into an all you can eat buffet restaurant costing £5 per head, and only eat one plate of food to the value of £5 and then leave?

The majority of you would say no because you would feel deprived, robbed or unfulfilled if you do not get more than your money's worth of food. Often this excess of food is usually beyond the boundaries of a simple meal, which would have cost the initial £5. You just could not do it.

Similarly, how would you feel if you attended a friend or family members wedding; all the trimming of the wedding was great, the brides dress, the groom, the outfits, the church and even the reception location was perfect, however you were served water and cucumber sandwiches, as much as you wanted or could eat or drink of either. Would it still be a great event to talk about for weeks? sharing the joy of the happy couple's nuptials? Or is the food a conversational piece for weeks on how disappointed the selection was or lack of selection as the case may be, would you say the food spoiled the wedding?

You may think this is a natural reaction to feel this way in both examples; however, this is just two of a few examples I share in the book to understand how we feel about food, our responses to it, its control over us and the freedoms we gain in other areas of our lives when we are set free from its bondages.

This book aims to deal with the lack a restraint some people have with food which causes many of their health problems and also how food can be used by the enemy of our souls as a doorway to introducing other indiscipline's within our lives.

This is not a diet book or a guide to health foods for the body, rather a look at food in its general sense and how we can be free of its hold over many of Gods people. A hold so deceptive that we may not even realise its effects on us until it is too late – and even then we may not have any idea it relates to our bad relationship with food.

I pray that the words on the pages of this book will help you in your Christian growth as you take a further step forward in your walk with Christ.

Remember big or small;

you are altogether beautiful, my love;

Songs of Solomon 4:7

Chapter 1: What is it all about?

Food is one of the main components to sustain human life, like air, we cannot live very long without it. We need food in order to survive, whether our lives are surrounded by it or we tend to shun it and only eat when necessary, it is something that no man can live without.

Wars have been fought over food like Tea and Sugar. In some circles of life, a person's status is determined by the quality of food they eat.

From the very opulent decadent meal served to kings to the humble 99p burger served to the man on a budget, food is everywhere and we cannot escape it.

In this chapter I want to take a look at what the bible tells us about food in its most general sense. I want to look at why we should not use food to judge those around us and get you to look at using this basic human requirement of food, with wisdom.

What should I eat?

Every moving thing that lives shall be food for you. And as I gave you the green plants, I give you everything.

Genesis 9:3

All food is good. This may be clear, but it is very rarely shared these days in churches.

There are those who preach that only certain animals with split hoofs and chew the cud should be eaten and every other meat is not to be consumed. However we must put this teaching from the Bible in context as this was an instruction to the Israelites.

There has to be balance as this kind of food advice is mainly relevant if you are planning to undertake all the rules given to the Israelites, which included the life style as well.

This kind of teaching comes with picking and choosing what is relevant and what is no longer relevant from the instructions given to the Israelites – so you must be very careful when following this kind of food consumption guide.

The point is not whether or not you agree to this kind of teaching and rules given to the Israelites, it is about how you conduct yourself and treat others who disagree with this position.

There are also those who take it upon themselves to demand as doctrine, that you should not consume certain foods. The reasons may be goods, but that does not mean it should become doctrine.

Timothy encourages us to be weary of teachings which tell us to avoid foods God has called good.

Now the Spirit expressly says that in later times some will depart from the faith by devoting themselves to deceitful spirits and teachings of demons…. …. who forbid marriage and require abstinence from foods that God created to be received with thanksgiving by those who believe and know the truth. For everything created by God is good, and nothing is to be rejected if it is received with thanksgiving, s for it is made holy by the word of God and prayer. 1Timothy 4:1-5

The Bible tells us that the foods we eat should not be an issue. We all have different taste and likes in food and we should receive it with thanksgiving. It is made holy by Gods Word and prayer.

I do not wish to focus on those who preach "do not eat this or that " however merely to say that there should be a clear difference between giving very good advice surrounding food and giving demands as doctrine concerning food. You must be careful not to preach what foods to abstain from as doctrine, or you can cause your brothers to stumble.

We should also know that in some countries certain foods are staples to the diet, some foods of which are not heard of or even consumed in other cultures.

And God said, "Behold, I have given you every plant yielding seed that is on the face of all the earth, and every tree with seed in its fruit. You shall have them for food.

Genesis 1:29

From the beginning, we have been given the freedom to eat and each food providing nutrients for the body as sustenance as God intended. Please note there was no exception made in this verse, it did not say except red fruit, or only very small seeds, God said "every", meaning all.

Do not judge others by the food they do or do not eat

Food for Thought

Although you are free to eat, we are encouraged to consider those around us who do not eat the same things, so we do not cause an offense. To go without pork for a week, while you stay at a friend's house is a small price to pay to show respect for their eating patterns or belief concerning pork.

Do not, for the sake of food, destroy the work of God. Everything is indeed clean, but it is wrong for anyone to make another stumble by what he eats. It is good not to eat meat or drink wine or do anything that causes your brother to stumble.

Romans 14:20-21

It is not for you to pass comment or judge the person because they do not like certain kinds of foods; in some cases, there are very good health reasons for an individual who avoid certain foods; or they have reasons not to like certain foods because of your personal upbringing or beliefs.

Romans 14:3 encourages us how not to act concerning our food choices. We are encouraged in the Word not to force our personal food choices and abstinences on others, or pass judgment against others by it.

If you no longer eat sugar, don't sit scornfully watching someone eating a chocolate cake.

The one who eats everything must not treat with contempt the one who does not, and the one who does not eat everything must not judge the one who does, for God has accepted them.

Romans 14:3

Food for Thought

Therefore do not let anyone judge you by what you eat or drink, or with regard to a religious festival, a New Moon celebration or a Sabbath day.

Colossians 2:16

When it comes to food you are free in Christ and therefore who he has set free, should not be judged or held in bondage over what they eat. Romans 14:3 tell us that God has accepted them both.

We must be careful not to judge one another by the food choices made.

The segregation within society can be seen greatly by the type of food people eat. You can travel to certain parts of your city and you will see more fast food takeaways in some areas where the economy is stretched and no fast food takeaways in other areas where there are higher levels of affluence, according to the demographic which live in those areas. You will rarely see many of those well know fast food shop in Chelsea or Dulwich Village.

The separation of food types and outlets in different areas brings a certain mind-set. The poor man rich man pattern start to appear. There is a mindset about people who live on fast food and cheap takeaways compared to someone who shops at Delis and high priced food stores. No matter how we try, food choices are used as a measuring stick against each of us. Whatever your choice or preference in food due to your area or class it does not make you stand better before God.

Food will not commend us to God. We are no worse off if we do not eat, and no better off if we do.

1 Corinthians 8:8

I stand by the fact that it is always good to share our knowledge on healthy body strengthening foods, but not to the point of judging another for not following the advice or the same chosen path.

Wisdom is the First thing Proverbs 4:7

Now I can hear all you healthy folk out there screaming at these pages, saying "how can you say all food is good? have you not seen the effects of starchy foods, sugars, fats, salt?"

Yes, I know and I hear you loud and clear, but let's remember the Word of God, all food is good.

All things are lawful [that is, morally legitimate, permissible], but not all things are beneficial or advantageous. All things are lawful, but not all things are constructive [to character] and edifying [to spiritual life].

(AMP)I Corinthians 10:23

The issue surrounding bad foods is the lack of knowledge and or restraint applied to those foods when taken. There are foods out there which are not good for us or beneficial, but we need wisdom and knowledge of these things.

My people are destroyed for lack of knowledge, because they have rejected knowledge

Hosea 4:6

Making our food choices require wisdom as well as understanding, something which is missing from many food selections.

Why wisdom? Because many people understand the harm fats, sugars and preservatives are doing to their body, but just cannot or don't care to stop.

I will cover the lack of restraint later in this book, but for now let us look at the use of wisdom and knowledge surrounding the foods we eat.

The beginning of wisdom is this: Get wisdom. Though it cost all you have, get understanding

Proverbs 4:7

It is good to walk in freedom when it comes to our eating; however this should not come at the cost of forsaking wisdom in what we should be putting into our bodies. Over the years, we have all acquired knowledge as to what foods are better for our health and our bodies. These will not be the same for all of us, as we are all different and certain foods react different within our bodies.

We are bombarded with TV shows, internet ads and well-wishers telling us about super foods and foods which strengthen the body and aid good health.

There are foods out there which aid our growth, physical strength and help in healing the body; these are foods which have been given and designed by God for the total well-being of our bodies.

We are also told about foods which cause the body harm due to their volume of use or their prolonged intake over the years. Foods containing harmful elements or hard to process ingredients and food which aid or cause many of the common diseases like diabetes are often known by many.

This knowledge in the hands of a Christian should steer you to be wise and focus on these foods which are better for the body and health and reduce the excesses of those foods which may harm the body.

Do you not know that your bodies are temples of the Holy Spirit, who is in you, whom you have received from God? You are not your own

Corinthians 6:19

Our bodies are not our own, they belong to God and house the Holy Spirit. As such we are to keep them well and free from sickness and disease where possible. We are to use wisdom. Yes, you are free to eat and put food in your body, but ultimately you are also responsible for the affects the foods you are putting into the body has on the body.

At your house, you are free to invite whoever you like into your home; a stranger cannot tell you who you should let into your home. However if a guest who you have let into your house, starts to destroy your things and behaves badly, it would make sense for you not to have that person in your home again, or if so, for the shortest time possible so they cause no damage at all.

This guest may behave themselves in other peoples home but not yours. So you would not continue to have them in for the sake of others.

This should be how we treat foods which do not behave well in our bodies. We are not all the same so foods which do not help your body, causing sickness, weight gain or bloating, may not act the same for someone else.

It is our responsibility to take care of this Temple which houses the Holy Spirit.

As Christians, we are to pray for health into our bodies and exercise our bodies, ensuring that what we put in our bodies does not counteract those prayers and exercise.

An example of your food counteracting your prayer and exercise would be you praying about a rash constantly appearing and causing you pain; when you know you have an allergy to particular foods you eat, causing the rash each time, and you refuse to stop eating it. This is not exercising wisdom concerning food.

This is where the food you are free to eat is hurting your body but you continue to eat it, and pray for healing at the same time – wisdom is needed.

Likewise, exercising to burn fat, and then going and eating something so high in fat that your body has put on 3 times more fat than you burned through the exercise – this is not exercising wisdom concerning food.

Food for Thought

The way of a fool is right in his own eyes, but a wise man listens to advise.

Proverbs 12:15

Although no one should dictate to you or judge you on what you eat, you should not forsake wisdom. If you have been given the knowledge of foods and how they can help your body, heal your body and strengthen your body, do not forsake good teaching.

The truth is if we really knew best and acted upon it we would not have as many of the illnesses and weaknesses that we see and spend so much time praying over in the church.

Let the wise hear and increase in learning and the one who understands obtain guidance

Proverbs 1:5

There should be no reason why anyone in this day and age cannot find the knowledge on the right foods for them. There are so many books, organizations, seminars and online articles which cover foods whatever your preference or choice of food may be. If you have not already done so; I would encourage, in all your getting, get wisdom.

So, whether you eat or drink, or whatever you do, do all to the glory of God.

1 Corinthians 10:31

Food for Thought

You are here to glorify God and for the glory of God to shine through you. This is not just on a Sunday morning or at a Christian event, but in everything you do.

In your walking, your talking and yes, even in your eating.

Food for Thought

Chapter 2: The Power of Food

When we consider something having power over us, we think of something big or strong. Maybe we will imagine something terrible and horrible which can control us and force our will, but rarely do we think of something good, pleasant and to be desired taking control over us or having a bad effect on us.

Food can persuade people to act, or respond to things they had no intention of acting upon. Sometimes these influences can be good and used to help and bring people together. Other times food can be used in a destructive way.

Every day they continued to meet together in the temple courts. They broke bread in their homes and ate together with glad and sincere hearts,

Acts 2:46

Food is not just a need for the human body, but a part of many cultural traditions and customs.

In fact every major Christian event is celebrated with food; like Easter and Christmas.

It is used in worship, festivals, events and general fellowship meetings.

Food is often used as a measure of the quality of functions. We should note the measurement is cultural and so unlikely understood by those outside of that culture.

For example, let's say you came from a culture where food is used to show appreciation of your guests at a wedding where the guest are lavished with meats, wines, breads and desserts, with large tables filled with snacks and delights in expectation of the main meal. You may get offended if you are invited to a wedding where you are served small finger food like vol-au-vents and crackers with caviar served on small trays.

We need to be mindful not to let our expectations of food affect our mood or attitude. I have seen people get very angry and upset when their food expectations are not met at a function.

Better is a dinner of herbs where love is than a fattened ox and hatred with it. Proverbs 15:17

It is better that you have the right atmosphere of love and appreciation, rather than the right food with the wrong feelings in the air.

In this chapter, we will look at how the food was influential and shaped certain events in the bible.

Food as an influence

In Jesus' day, we read what happened when the wine ran out at a wedding. The food was such an integral part of the wedding, it became a stressful thing for the hosts when the wine had finished.

The third day a wedding took place at Cana in Galilee. Jesus' mother was there, and Jesus and his disciples had also been invited to the wedding. When the wine was gone, Jesus' mother said to him, "They have no more wine."......... His mother said to the servants, "Do whatever he tells you".......... Jesus said to the servants, "Fill the jars with water"; so they filled them to the brim. Then he told them, "Now draw some out and take it to the master of the banquet." They did so and the master of the banquet tasted the water that had been turned into wine. He did not realize where it had come from though the servants who had drawn the water knew. Then he called the bridegroom aside and said, "Everyone brings out the choice wine first and then the cheaper wine after the guests have had too much to drink, but you have saved the best till now.

John 2 1-10

The comments from the guest when they tasted the wine made by Jesus showed how much attention the guests paid to the food.

Let's consider what is more important here, is it more important to be invited to the wedding or given cake from the wedding you were not invited too?

It is important to remember why we are at these functions and remember the food is just an accompaniment to enhance the event.

Although we should accept that food is a good tool for fellowship and events, we must be careful however, not to make food so important to us, that we lose the main reason and focus for the gathering.

This happened to the church in Corinth where the presence of food for the lord Supper was abused and became the focus.

So then, when you come together, it is not the Lord's Supper you eat, for when you are eating, some of you go ahead with your own private suppers. As a result, one person remains hungry and another gets drunk. Don't you have homes to eat and drink in?

1 Corinthians 11:20 – 22

It is fine to present food at functions but unless it is the reason for the event, we must be careful not to lose focus or appreciation for the event. The food in the scripture quoted was a representation used for the remembrance of Christ and what he has done for us, but this was soon forgotten.

The power of food to make changes

She went and told the man of God, and he said, "Go, sell the oil and pay your debts. You and your sons can live on what is left."

2 Kings 4:7

In this scripture we see how food was used to bring about deliverance. In this story it produced life-long revenue. It was also used as multiplication of a resource used for another widow's deliverance through a difficult time as read in the next scripture.

For this is what the LORD, the God of Israel, says: 'The jar of flour will not be used up and the jug of oil will not run dry until the day the LORD sends rain on the land. 'She went away and did as Elijah had told her. So there was food every day for Elijah and for the woman and her family. For the jar of flour was not used up and the jug of oil did not run dry, in keeping with the word of the LORD spoken by Elijah.

1 Kings 17:14-16

In both these scriptures we see how food can be used to bring about a significant change to our lives and circumstances when placed in the hand of God.

The vehicle of food can be used to bring fellowship, Love and blessings when used in the right way and when anointed it can bring a miracle like the two occasions we have just read.

Sadly however not all miracles performed with food lead to the seeking of more of God and his glory, but rather the seeking of more food.

Many people who followed Jesus witnessed miracles performed with food when Jesus fed over 5000 people on two occasions.

On one occasion, the focus on food became so strong that the crowd of over 5000 came back for more, rather than the Word.

Jesus answered, "Very truly I tell you, you are looking for me, not because you saw the signs I performed but because you ate the loaves and had your fill

John 6:26

The word and the miracles Jesus performed became overshadowed by the free and no doubt tasty food provided. I can only imagine if the wine Jesus made at the wedding stirred up a great response, then the food Jesus blessed and multiplied must have tasted great.

So much so, that they pursued Jesus after the feeding. Jesus said, it was the pursuit of the food, not the miracles that brought them back again.

The Messenger Bible puts it like this; *Jesus answered, "You've come looking for me not because you saw God in my actions but because I fed you, filled your stomachs—and for free.*

You may think this makes little sense, why would they forsake the Word, or the Miracles for food.

Think about it like this, you are invited to a friend's birthday party at a restaurant you have never been to before; you attend and they serve you your meal. The food is delicious, so tasty, that it enhances the event.

After the party has ended, you are still thinking about the great quality of the food. You are not thinking about the birthday person or next year when you can celebrate with them again – your thoughts are taken up with visiting the restaurant again.

You're not so concerned about the presence of the birthday person, you're just happy to go back; maybe with a different group of friends or family.

You even offer the venue to anyone who is looking for a place to hold an event.

What has happened here, the food has become more memorable than the people you were there to meet and celebrate the birthday with.

It is this thinking which had the 5000 plus pursue Jesus. They may have been there for the Word and the miracles, staying until they were hungry, but they gathered again for the food.

Drawn away from Gods will

Be alert and of sober mind. Your enemy the devil prowls around like a roaring lion looking for someone to devour

1 Peter 5:8

The enemy of our soul is walking around seeking those who he can destroy; one of the primary ways he does this is by food.

Why with food?

Food is something we need, whoever you are, no matter how strong you are.

If the devil can get you to open yourselves up to a bad relationship with food, he can get a foothold in your life.

Now the serpent was more crafty than any other beast of the field that the LORD God had made. He said to the woman, "Did God actually say, 'You shall not eat of any tree in the garden'?" And the woman said to the serpent, "We may eat of the fruit of the trees in the garden, but God said, 'You shall not eat of the fruit of the tree that is in the midst of the garden, neither shall you touch it, lest you die.'" but the serpent said to the woman, "You will not surely die. for God knows that when you eat of it your eyes will be opened, and you will be like God, knowing good and evil." So when the woman saw that the tree was good for food, and that it was a delight to the eyes, and that the tree was to be desired to make one wise, she took of its fruit and ate, and she also gave some to her husband who was with her, and he ate.

Genesis 3:1-6

We read how the food became the vehicle used for disobedience. It is clear to note that it was not hunger that drew Eve to eat, it was to gain something good, to be like God and therefore the food became desirous to the eyes.

After such a successful plan of using food, the Devil tried it again with the second Adam, Jesus.

The Devil knew Jesus was disciplined and would not succumb to the desire of this world. However the Devil knew Jesus had to eat like everyone else to survive. So once again, something we need was used to deliver indiscipline.

Then Jesus was led up by the Spirit into the wilderness to be tempted by the devil. And after fasting forty days and forty nights, he was hungry. And the tempter came and said to him, "If you are the Son of God, command these stones to become loaves of bread." But he answered, "It is written, "'Man shall not live by bread alone, but by every word that comes from the mouth of God.'"

Matthew 4:1-4

As we know the story of Jesus, the second Adam did not succumb to the temptation of food like the first Adam.

What is also good to note is that, unlike the first Adam, Jesus was hungry, so there were two victories which took place here; the victory of the fast which we cover later on in the chapter and the victory of the Word of God in action over the desire of the flesh.

God has plans and purposes for our lives, with food. Those plans cannot be enacted as the disciplines and walls of self-control have been removed. These broken walls are granting access to other forms or indiscipline's within the life of the Christian.

Sometimes the desires of the body are so great it makes you lose focus.

Once when Jacob was cooking stew, Esau came in from the field, and he was exhausted. And Esau said to Jacob, "Let me eat some of that red stew, for I am exhausted!" (Therefore, his name was called Edom.) Jacob said "Sell me your birthright now." Esau said, "I am about to die; of what use is a birth right to me?" Jacob said, "Swear to me now." So he swore to him and sold his birth right to Jacob. Then Jacob gave Esau bread and lentil stew, and he ate and drank and rose and went his way. Thus Esau despised his birth right.

Genesis 25:29 – 34

Esau allowed the hunger to cause him to lose sight of the bigger promise.

Discipline is doing something today that will benefit you tomorrow.

Had Esau considered his tomorrow he would have thought twice about his actions that day, he did not consider his future, and the same is for those who have a bad relationship with food.

The truth be known, Esau would not have died if he missed one evening meal. None of us will, but we have been through that feeling of, "I don't care, I need to eat"

See to it that no one fails to obtain the grace of God; that no "root of bitterness" springs up and causes trouble, and by it many become defiled; that no one is sexually immoral or unholy like Esau, who sold his birth right for a single meal. For you know that afterward when he desired to inherit the blessing, he was rejected, for he found no chance to repent though he sought it with tears.

Hebrew 12:16-18

That act of giving into his hunger pangs made him make a silly choice. This is also true today, as many are in places they do not want to be in their life and their health due to what they did in the past, and still doing concerning food and their health.

Jacob saw the power of food and even used it again when he followed his mother's instructions to trick the first son blessing from his Father in Genesis 27 was not the only time food was used to deceive. It was used to deceive a prophet and get him to lose out on his blessing in 1st Kings 13:18

These scriptures have been used to help show you not to underestimate the power of food to draw someone out of their rightful place in God and lose sight of what matters.

Fasting

One way you get closer to God and hear clear direction for your life is through fasting from food.

Fasting has changed over the years, from total abstinence from food mentioned in the Bible to a partial absence from food called an intermittent fast.

Food has caused the dependency upon itself through our desires. One major sickness affecting fasting is diabetes caused by food sugar levels. It means that a diabetic on a fast will need to allow small breaks for food intake.

"And when you fast, do not look gloomy like the hypocrites, for they disfigure their faces that their fasting may be seen by others. Truly, I say to you, they have received their reward. But when you fast, anoint your head and wash your face, that your fasting may not be seen by others but by your Father who is in secret. And your Father who sees in secret will reward you.

Matthew 6:16-18

There are set conditions when we break from food and choose to fast. It is not just taking that time out to pray and seek God but it is a total abstinence from food.

When there is a bad relationship with food, it is harder to do a fast and so we introduce partial fasts.

This is usually done so that the hunger pangs do not distract us, or we do not start to feel faint.

Strangely enough, there is little talk of the God of the fast and his power to supernaturally sustain us during a fast. Maybe because we are driven by our senses and do not rely on Gods power to accomplish something we see as natural rather than supernatural.

Fasting is often seen as willingness to abstain from food for a set time. When observed with this view, the word fast becomes a general term and therefore is undertaken using general methods.

However, in the Bible we read of fasts which were total abstinence from food and drink and a complete inner focus on God, or the spiritual matter at hand.

I ate no delicacies, no meat or wine entered my mouth, nor did I anoint myself at all, for the full three weeks.

Daniel 10:3

And the people of Nineveh believed God. They called for a fast ..... "By the decree of the king and his nobles: Let neither man nor beast, herd nor flock, taste anything. Let them not feed or drink water

Jonah 3:5-9

So he was there with the Lord forty days and forty nights. He neither ate bread nor drank water.

Exodus 34:28

I would encourage you to take time out of your routine to fast. It is great for spiritual growth and as an additional blessing it offers great mental and physical benefits to the body.

There are benefits you cannot get from an intermittent fasting, where you do half a day at a time (under 13 hours).

Some of the reported health benefits from a fast lasting more than one day (over 24 hours) are;

- Natural burning of excess body fat after 8 hours

- The body detoxifies itself from toxins stored in fat
- Higher endorphin "feel Good" hormones are released after three days into the fast.
- Healthy blood cells are produced faster

The USC News research on Cancer found that fasting triggers stem cell regeneration of damaged, old immune system in cancer patients.

In June 2015 the Daily Telegraph published new findings from USC which said that these short fasts are not accomplishing much, and to get real benefits from a fast you need to do it for at least 5 days straight.

A Sky news report in April 2015 claimed that regular fasting lasting over 13 hours have proven to extend a person's life.

A leading Doctor in Human Biology claimed that over 50% of sickness could be solved by reducing calorie intake, with a higher volume of complete recovery through a fast.

There are countless health benefits experienced in fasting which sadly for some may never be achieved as they lack the discipline to sustain abstinence from food so the benefits gained for more than a day is very rarely achieved.

I would suggest you learn more about the power gained through a fast, as well as the benefits it has on your body.

Food for Thought

There are countless materials out their which can assist you in your spiritual growth, and even Doctors advice to help you on the physical health side as well.

It is a good thing to fast regularly.

Chapter 3: Addictions

No temptation has overtaken you that is not common to man. God is faithful, and he will not let you be tempted beyond your ability, but with the temptation he will also provide the way of escape, that you may be able to endure it.

1 Corinthians 10:13

The dictionary says the word addiction means The act or condition of being addicted to a particular substance or activity.

Addictions can take three shapes;

- Emotional, where you feel you need it;
- Physical, where it is something chemical, and bodily
- Psychological, where mentally you truly believe in its need

Where there are no boundaries, you find bondage.

It is important to know not all addictions are destructive, but they all require boundaries.

An example of this, is a person addicted to exercise. It is a good thing to focus ones energy on, but if boundaries are not placed around it, then you can actually cause yourself harm.

Where you don't restrict yourself, or limit yourself, you find yourself in bondage to that thing.

Although we are talking about food, the rules I give below will apply to all kinds of addictions.

- Seriously look at your need for the thing.
- Consider where the need came from. For example do you need it because you feel low, or was told by someone it is what you needed.
- What do you associate with the addiction? For example, joy when eating chocolate, or calm when smoking.
- Be aware of it, log or write down as many, if not all the time you do it, eat it etc.
- Consider what you can do or use to replace it. For example, chewing gum to replace smoking, or eating regularly so that you are not given to excess when meal times come round.

There are many other things which can be done, but I believe these will give you a good start.

Be not among drunkards or among gluttonous eaters of meat, [21] for the drunkard and the glutton will come to poverty, and slumber will clothe them with rags

Proverbs 23:20 -21

Often when we think about addictions we focus on things like drugs and alcohol. If someone says food addictions we think of someone oversized with health problems.

Rarely do we think of gluttony. Gluttony is simply to overeat. You do not have to be large in size to take part in excess.

There are also those who under eat to their own hurt, who we also need to consider when we think of a bad relationship with food.

If someone overeats and does this continually, they are labelled as a glutton.

There are TV shows where people have eating challenges to see how much they can consume within a short time, which is accepted entertainment, yet if it was someone doing the same thing with alcohol we would be alarmed and view the show as some sort of abuse and think of their poor liver.

If you are at an all you can eat restaurant; it would not make the act right. If you feel that you are at liberty to eat as much as you can because you are at an all you can buffet, this is wrong. It does not justify the act of overeating.

Let me put it another way, would you be so accepting of an all you can drink beer or wine bar?

If we say the place makes the actions of over eating acceptable by the fact it encourages you to "eat as much as you can"; then is Adultery acceptable as long as it is done in a brothel, or gambling OK as long as it's done at a betting shop? – Of course not. These are extreme examples, but you get my point.

With this all you can get dining is a mentality which says, "it's free I must have more". There is a sense of loss or bargain felt.

- Loss

If you asked someone to pay £5 for a buffet but asked them to only have one plate of food, there is a sense of loss, you want as much as you can get for as little as you can get it. In reality, if you were to pay for that one plate of food separately from a menu and not on a buffet, you would see you have paid half price for that one plate of food.

However you will feel deprived if you do not go back for more. This would make sense if you had paid £50 and not eaten the value of your fee.

- Bargain

The joy of getting something for almost nothing, that bargain mentality which kicks in to say, if it's free, or cheap, I'm there.

If you think the food is not that big of an issue, consider the Word of God which regards the excess or the greed for food in line with those who are drunkards.

For the drunkard and the glutton will come to poverty, and slumber will clothe them with rags. Proverbs 23:21

Proverbs says that the glutton will eat till they are tired, how many times have you eaten till you are so full that you can just fall asleep where you sit.

Another translation of rags is their clothes become unwearable, that's not just for the drunkard but that also means your clothes become pulled out, too small to get into them for the glutton.

Although drink is mentioned often in the Bible, my focus is not on the excess of alcohol, because strong drink is a different entrapment.

What do I mean by a different entrapment? Not everyone drinks alcohol, there are those like myself who dislike the taste, others do not drink for their belief or health reasons – it is a thing which can be abused and enslaves many, but unlike food, we do not all need it. We can live without it, so the relevance of its snare will not capture all of us.

But strong drink is a trap used by the devil and should not be taken lightly in any way.

Show moderation

Nor thieves, nor the greedy, nor drunkards, nor revilers, nor swindlers will inherit the kingdom of God.

1Corinthians 6:10

The kingdom of God is Gods rules, Gods way of doing things. You cannot enter his way of doing things with the absence of discipline or self-control in the things you do. You cannot live in excess having a wrong relationship with food and inherit Gods kingdom, when his kingdom rule teaches restraint; the Kingdom mind-set is not that of loss or freebies.

It is not good to eat much honey, nor is it glorious to seek one's own glory.

Proverbs 25:37

If you are like me with a sweet tooth, you could live on sugary foods every day. We are advised to cut back on the sweet stuff. Wisdom would be to follow good instructions, especially if it's coming from the Word of God

For many, of whom I have often told you and now tell you even with tears, walk as enemies of the cross of Christ. Their end is destruction, their god is their belly,

Philippians 3:18 -19

Where the verse says their God is their bellies, it means they are driven by their desires, which include those desire of the physical belly.

Show restraint and put a knife to your throat if you are given to appetite.

Proverbs 23:2

Do not let your desire rule you so much that you become enslaved to food and what you eat. If you had to stop eating a certain food for a while or stop dining out for a while do you see it as a sense of loss? Are you driven by your appetite? Being given to your appetite causes harm to your body and your health

"Food is meant for the stomach and the stomach for food"—and God will destroy both one and the other. The body is not meant for sexual immorality, but for the Lord, and the Lord for the body.

I Corinthians 6:13

The stomach and food are all perishable and can be destroyed. Put your energy to that which is eternal and brings a greater blessing – we are reminded again that the body is the Lords.

One who is full loathes honey, but to one who is hungry everything bitter is sweet.

Proverbs 27: 7

Don't let yourself get hungry before you eat. Like Esau you can lose perspective driven by your hunger. As the scripture says, even something bitter, something wrong for your health, or bad for you, or just not needed for your body, will be eaten because you let yourself get to the point of unreasonable desires, you let yourself get hungry.

When you are full, you should stop eating.

If you have found honey, eat only enough for you, lest you have your fill of it and vomit it.

Proverbs 25:16

You can enjoy a good thing without taking it to excess. Overeating is never seen as an acceptable thing.

Do you not know that you are God's temple and that God's Spirit dwells in you? If anyone destroys God's temple, God will destroy him. For God's temple is holy, and you are that temple.

1 Corinthians 3:16-17

We are given the responsibility of taking care of this body, which means we need to consider the things we put into it which may affect our health. Also, the excesses or lack of foods which cause the many issues we see in the world and in the church around our physical bodies.

We are held into account of how we treat this Temple, not just how others treat us.

Do not be deceived: God is not mocked, for whatever one sows, that will he also reap. For the one who sows to his own flesh will from the flesh reap corruption, but the one who sows to the Spirit will from the Spirit reap eternal life.

Galatians 6:7-8

If we give into our fleshly desires, we will reap those rewards, and the rewards of giving into these desires are never good or helpful for the body, even though the body craves it.

Chapter 4: Exercise

For while bodily training is of some value, godliness is of value in every way, as it holds promise for the present life and also for the life to come.

1 Timothy 4:8

Exercising is a vital part of the healthy journey, albeit a necessary part and often forgotten. Here we are reminded that it has its value.

Beloved, I pray that all may go well with you and that you may be in good health, as it goes well with your soul.

3 John 1:2

If we do not exercise our bodies, we can never claim to be in good health.

As society changes, natural exercise like walking, lifting, running and bending are removed and replaced with industry and cars and effortless comforts. So much so that you can live for years without performing the simplest of exercises to the natural body.

But I discipline my body and keep it under control, lest after preaching to others I myself should be disqualified.

1 Corinthians 9:27

It takes effort to stay healthy in exercise. Paul said he had to apply discipline to bring his body under control. It was not gained from doing nothing.

Don't wait for the desire to come upon you to exercise, as the bodily desires are to do as little as possible and gain the greatest rewards. We need to take action beyond the natural desire to get the body moving and break a sweat.

1st Timothy 4:8 tells us that it is not just exercise needed for us to be healthy, but what goes on inside our bodies makes us fully healthy.

Exercise is something that is needful for the body. There are those who see exercise as a chore and something grueling, but not all exercise has to be military style; it can be as simple as a long walk or an hour of gardening.

Exercise means to work the body. This can be done in many ways. Way before dance routines and gyms ever came about we were told to exercise.

There were also harder exercises which athletes and soldiers performed, as mentioned by Paul in the Bible.

Our bodies are designed for movement, legs for walking, arms for holding and lifting. Cars, public transport and TV are the highest attackers to our general physical movement.

Exercise is not a counterbalance to bad eating. You know the "I'll eat this bad food now and then work it of later". It is to make us fitter and healthier, not to make room for our food excesses. The "I'll stay longer at the gym as I'm eating out tomorrow" tools.

The body is often used visually to decide our well-being. This means as long as we are not too large or too small for our desired height and weight then we are ok.

At the beginning of every year we are bombarded with TV ads, telling us of a new diet or workout to reduce our size, the visual aspect.

This means that someone with a bad relationship with food will think they are ok if they are not overweight or underweight, especially when exercise is keeping them from the visual tells.

2nd Corinthians 6:19 – 20 tells us that our body is not our own. We need to consider how we treat our body on the inside, and not only consider how it looks on the outside. Exercise is often used as a concealer.

If you were to stop exercising, what would happen on the outside based on your intake?

The Bible encourages us to take care of our physical bodies. It is sad however that if someone is not, we do not mention it, unless it is affecting their health.

In many churches, Christians would sooner teach on sexual immorality than exercise or gluttony. It's a side note, not a main point it would seem.

I am not saying you cannot use exercise to deal with your health, but if the eating is not dealt with as well, it will show on the outside.

Using exercise to counter balance bad eating shows itself when exercise ceases, maybe due to injury or a change of life, the weight gain is above normal as the fence of exercise comes down.

3rd John 1:2 we are encouraged by the Word to be whole, to focus on getting our body, health, eating in line with our soul, which should also be well.

Our soul is our thoughts and emotions. We are encouraged to bring our health, which covers exercise and food, into harmony as our soul is in harmony.

Note, we are not encouraged to get our health in place before our souls, because we need to change what goes on within, before we can show what's happening without. We cover more of this point in chapter 6.

Chapter 5: Inner Desires

*Since you died with Christ to the basic principles of this world, why,
as though you still belonged to it, do you submit to its rules: "Do not
handle! Do not taste! Do not touch!"? These are all destined to perish
with use, because they are based on human commands and teachings.
Such regulations indeed have an appearance of wisdom, with their
self-imposed worship, their false humility and their harsh treatment of
the body, but they lack any value in restraining sensual indulgence.*

Colossians 2:20-23

Many of us believe if we think really hard and try hard we
can get a hold on our bad relationship with food. Let me
say, all diets work when followed exactly to the letter,
where no medical conditions apply.

However if it was as simple as following healthy rules like
a diet, then there would be no issue surrounding a bad
relationship with food. However the truth be known,
following a good diet, or a bad one does not deal with the
real issues.

Colossians tells us that the Holy Spirit is there to guide us in
all things, yet we follow the rules of this world, which does
not deal with our inner desires.

Statistics show over 95% of people who go on diets put the
weight back on, with 75% gaining more weight. That means
less that one in ten people are successful in the long term,
when following these rules.

For example, if you are a chocoholic, for you to follow a
diet, the basic rules would be for you to keep away from

chocolate or eat an alternative to the chocolate. You are told to remove it from your home and you are encouraged not to walk down the confectionary food aisle.

Although this advice is good in essence, it does not deal with how you feel about chocolate and behave around it.

Through the Holy Spirit, Paul is saying in this verse, you have the power to walk down a confectionary aisle without it bothering you, also having chocolate in your home and possessing the self-control to not eat it or too much of it.

Isn't that great? Being able to walk down an aisle which sells your favourite foods, the same way you walk down the green vegetable aisle?

Now I am not talking about mind control like hypnosis, which makes you dislike certain foods, so you feel free around them. I am talking about still liking those foods you have an issue with, but being able to control yourself around them. Having the ability to think and act according to the Holy Spirit guiding you, telling you, "not now", "never again", or "you've had enough".

In researching for this book I've noticed there was a feeling in those who felt deprived of the food they loved, or robbed of pleasure if they could not give into their desires. Their desires were saying "I have to eat this now".

To deny yourself from what you want to eat now, feels like a punishment, rather than a reward.

To be told no, or not now by the Holy Spirit needs to be welcomed with, he knows what's best for you, rather than, the feelings of being deprived.

The issue here is dealing with one's inner desires, not just the outward actions.

Over 95% of people who go on diets regain the weight, as it becomes hard to continue without the rules there in front of them to tell them eat, don't eat, start or stop. The boredom of the same foods and eating what's best kicks in.

Jesus came to give us Grace from Legalism. The question is asked then, how does the Holy Spirit help me to have a better relationship with food without following rules and a diet plan?

Let me address the question; it is not a bad thing to follow a diet, but that cannot be all there is to your relationship with food.

The Holy Spirit brings Self-Control, which is a fruit of the Spirit. This is something hard to get without the Holy Spirit, because with his help, The Holy Spirit helps you to build disciplines which deals with your inner feeling towards food, not just your outward ability to follow a set of rules.

For this very reason, make every effort to supplement your faith with virtue, and virtue with knowledge, and knowledge with self-control, and self-control with steadfastness, and steadfastness with godliness, and godliness with brotherly affection, and brotherly affection with love.

2 Peter 1:5-7

Let's read this verse again with additions to help us visualize the help we seek.

*For this very reason, make every effort to supplement your faith with virtue **(good values like eating right)**, and virtue with knowledge **(Knowing the good food we need for our body)**, and knowledge with self-control **(The God given ability to say no to the wrong foods or limit their intake)**, and self-control with steadfastness **(remaining constant so this is a lifetime practice and habit - Disciplined)**, and steadfastness with godliness, and godliness with brotherly affection, and brotherly affection with love.*

Self-Control

But the fruit of the Spirit is love, joy, peace, patience, kindness, goodness, faithfulness, gentleness, self-control; against such things there is no law.

Galatians 5:22-23

Self-Control is a spiritual fruit given by the Holy Spirit. Remember we are talking about the Spirit, from the inside out.

You may be thinking, I know a lot of people who are not Christians and so do not have the Holy Spirit, yet they show great self-control.

You could then say you do not need the Holy Spirit to have self-control.

Well let's take a look at what self-control means; the ability to control oneself, in particular one's emotions and desires in difficult situations.

Self-Control outside of the Holy Spirit controls the outer behaviour only. You can be screaming on the inside, yet acting very calm. The Holy Spirit works from inside out.

Another difference is that we all have different desires, they are not the same. I mentioned in an earlier chapter I have a sweet tooth; my husband does not.

He does not need self-control to stop him from eating something he does not desire, or can take or leave from one day to the next.

Self-control is the ability to control oneself in the face of emotional temptation on the inside, not just the outside. If the situation is not a temptation for you or a difficult situation for you, then the control you show in the face of it, is your lack of desire to act in that situation.

We often look on those with a good relationship with food and wonder, I wish I liked the foods they like with all those healthy choices, but the truth be known, we are all different and have different desires and should not wish to be like anyone else.

So, can we have self-control apart from God the Holy Spirit?

For God gave us a spirit not of fear but of power and love and self-control.

2 Timothy 1:7

It is God that gives us the ability to use self-Control when the occasion arises; we do not all take advantage of what we have been given.

That ability to act and do the right thing, control oneself in the face of difficulties. The Holy Spirit gets us to think clearly in that given situation to control ourselves.

A mind that thinks clearly and can control their choices is given by God, a sober mind. Here in the next scripture Peter refers to both self-control and a sober mind concerning our prayers

The end of all things is at hand; therefore being self-controlled and sober-minded for the sake of your prayers.

1 Peter 4:7

.A man without self-control is like a city broken in two and left without walls.

Proverbs 25:28

The control which comes from God, works from the inside out by the control given by the Holy Spirit.

If we cannot gain self-control within our lives, we fall into bondage to anything that comes our way which the flesh desires.

But I say, walk by the Spirit, and you will not gratify the desires of the flesh. For the desires of the flesh are against the Spirit, and the desires of the Spirit are against the flesh, for these are opposed to each other, to keep you from doing the things you want to do.

Galatians 5:16 -17

When you allow the Holy Spirit in your life to grow self-control within your life, you will seek the things of the Spirit rather than giving into the flesh.

For the weapons of our warfare are not of the flesh but have divine power to destroy strongholds. We destroy arguments and every lofty opinion raised against the knowledge of God, and take every thought captive to obey Christ,

2 Corinthians 10:4-5

You cannot fight this on your own; you cannot break free if you fight in the flesh only

Change to self-control will be through a changed mind. From the inside out, is how this becomes achieved.

Every athlete exercises self-control in all things. They do it to receive a perishable wreath, but we an imperishable.

1 Corinthians 9:25

Self-control is needed in our eating, our exercises and every part of our lives where we are taken in fleshly desires.

Do not be deceived: "Bad company ruins good morals.

1 Corinthians 15:33

Remember where you practice your self-control. If you are not a donor in the company you keep, you are the recipients, be mindful of what company you keep in all things.

Do not willingly walk into temptations where you do not have self-control.

<u>The anointing of Discipline</u>

You may feel we have just covered this area in self-control but it is a different subject matter.

You can have self-control without discipline, but you cannot have discipline without self-control.

Where self-control is doing the right thing, although faced with the opportunity of doing the wrong thing - discipline is a trained mind set, a predetermined and transformed behavior you chose to stand on to reach a goal, desire or path in life.

For example, where self-control through the Holy Spirit provides restraint in the face of temptation, discipline is a life style and pattern which allows us to walk away from the very presence of the temptation, changing how you even view the temptation.

Another example would be like this; You are in a hurry and need to cross the road, the lights have not changed to green for you to cross, but there happen to be no cars around and the road is clear,

Self-control will stop you from crossing even though you want to.

Discipline only wants to cross when the light turns green.

The self-controlled only man keeps his eye on the traffic and therefore needs to control himself from crossing when things look clear.

The disciplined man keeps his eyes on the light and is not tempted to cross until he sees the lights changed.

When the bible talks about discipline, it is about changing the mind-set and transforming the mind so it says, only cross when the man turns green.

Its teaching someone the right rules, so the right path are ingrained in their thoughts and their behaviour.

When you discipline a child, you are teaching them to behave a different way to the way they are acting. You are sowing new information inside of them so that what comes out is as a natural course.

For the moment all discipline seems painful rather than pleasant, but later it yields the peaceful fruit of righteousness to those who have been trained by it.

Hebrew 12:11

Over time it becomes natural and our goal is gained, better health, better choices. Be open to renewing your mind till the new way becomes your only way, and it becomes the way.

But I discipline my body and keep it under control, lest after preaching to others I myself should be disqualified.

2 Corinthians 9:27

It will take discipline to stay on track and apply the Word taught to you so you are not found a hearer of the Word only.

> *"Behold, blessed is the one whom God reproves; therefore despise not the discipline of the Almighty.*

> *Job 5:17*

Welcome discipline, as it helps you shape up and teaches you the right way. You cannot be disciplined if you are not being corrected from the wrong way and taught or shown the right way.

> *Know then in your heart that, as a man disciplines his son, the Lord your God disciplines you.*

> *Deuteronomy 8:5*

As a man tells his son he is wrong in his actions and tells him the right way he should behave, act, speak etc., so God does this to us so we behave, act and speak right – and eat right.

To correct and bring in line to a transformed way of thinking, that way of thinking incorporates self-control

> *Share in suffering as a good soldier of Christ Jesus. No soldier gets entangled in civilian pursuits, since his aim is to please the one who enlisted him. An athlete is not crowned unless he competes according to the rules.*

> *2 Timothy 2:3-5*

When you are disciplined in a thing your mind set changes as your goals change. Those who change to healthy way of living seek a greater reward and their focus is on attaining that goal.

If you are disciplined, you cannot fall off the wagon as it is the way you think and the way you have become.

I remember watching a TV show about monks in a monastery who were disciplined. They had strict teachings, followed stricter rules and conformed to the teaching they were given around them.

However, during the programme it mentioned how some had chosen to leave the Monastery and leave the ways of a monk. Some of the disciplines they had been taught went completely.

The reason for this was that in the monastery they practiced their self-control and discipline in a place where there was no temptation, no strong drink, women, gold or silver for greed, and their food were served to them as portion controlled meals.

For many of them leaving the monastery, the strength they thought they had, was not really there.

They had never crossed a road to appreciate waiting for the green walk sign.

Living in the Monastery for some was like crossing open roads where there are no lights to turn red and say, do not walk.

It is interesting to note that Christ called us to be Disciples and not Christians.

Disciple means "a disciplined one"

Chapter 6: Legalism vs Grace

Many of us have always lived by rules, a tick list of do's and don'ts in order to keep us in line.

The problem with living by the laws of do's and do not's is we try and fail consistently. This is because the inner desires are still there; we crave for a thing inside which eventually show to the outside. We then fall off the wagon.

The thing about the law is it is something to follow quickly in no time and for those who want to get it done without delay. The thought of change by grace taking time and requiring effort puts many people off. Society is full of those who prefer a quick fix,

Legalism is living according to rules laid out in the Bible.

You are not being asked to move from the worldly rules of do's and don'ts onto a biblical set of dos and don'ts.

These people honor me with their lips, but their hearts are far from me. They worship me in vain; their teachings are but rules taught by men. –

Matthew 15: 8-9

Hear we read how God was not pleased that he had the people's action but he did not have their heart.

As mentioned in the previous chapters, it is about transformation on the inside rather than change in action on the outside only. Do's and don'ts only deal with the outside.

The reason legalism does not work is outlined in the next passage

Then Jesus spoke to the crowds and to His disciples, saying: "The scribes and the Pharisees have seated themselves in the chair of Moses; therefore all that they tell you, do and observe, but do not do according to their deeds; for they say things and do not do them." They tie up heavy burdens and lay them on men's shoulders, but they themselves are unwilling to move them with so much as a finger. –

Matthew 23: 1-4

It is not that the law was not good, but it provided the opportunity to do wrong.

Legalism is a very natural way of living, but it is not sustainable. The scribes were not able to live in accordance with all the strict rules they had been requesting of the people, and why? Because they had not dealt with the inner desires and therefore the proverbial draw of chocolate was always present.

So how does this differ from Grace?

Grace deals with the heart of the person, working on your inner desires.

Jesus gives the difference between legalism and grace in the Sermon on the Mount

"You have heard that it was said to the people long ago, 'Do not murder, and anyone who murders will be subject to judgment.' But I tell you that anyone who is angry with his brother will be subject to judgment. -

Matthew 5: 21-22

The flesh is never worthy, grace gives us something that we do not deserve and never could earn.

Whoever is slow to anger is better than the mighty, and he who rules his spirit than he who takes a city.

Proverbs 16:32

If you can gain control on the inner workings of your spirit and be ruled by them, then you are greater than one who can merely do the external actions.

But he said to me, "My grace is sufficient for you, for my power is made perfect in weakness." Therefore I will boast all the more gladly of my weaknesses, so that the power of Christ may rest upon me.

2 Corinthians 12:9

It is in our weaknesses when we let go that we can allow grace to take over and work within us

For sin will have no dominion over you, since you are not under law but under grace.

Romans 6:14

You are not under rules of do's and don'ts but under the guidance of grace which deals with the inside; how we feel and react to a thing.

The law does not deal with the inside so you continue to crave or long for something you should not have. Grace deals with the feeling and longing inside so that you walk a stronger walk and journey

But if it is by grace, it is no longer on the basis of works; otherwise grace would no longer be grace.

Romans 11:6

Under grace it is no longer you on your own bringing your deliverance and success, but the workings of God through grace in your life

You do not sit back and do nothing now that you have grace; it is done by grace through you.

But by the grace of God I am what I am, and his grace toward me was not in vain. On the contrary, I worked harder than any of them, though it was not I, but the grace of God that is with me.

1 Corinthians 15:10

Grace in your lives does not mean you do less, in fact you accomplish more.

Let us then with confidence draw near to the throne of grace, that we may receive mercy and find grace to help in time of need.

Hebrews 4:16

So how do you get grace or more of it in times of need and temptation? We draw need to him, that simple.

For example, if you are being drawn into something you should not be or tempted and you take the time to stop and pray or seek God for grace, you have immediately focused on something else.

In the time taken to seek God, you have drawn near in prayer and scriptures. You receive grace to overcome that situation.

The truth is, many people do not turn to God until after the temptation has passed or during, but rarely is it the first action.

And from his fullness we have all received, grace upon grace.

John 1:16

This is not just for the few, this is something that we all have received and have access to, the question is are you willing to draw near for more or is it too much effort.

But grow in the grace and knowledge of our Lord and Savior Jesus Christ. To him be the glory both now and to the day of eternity. Amen.

2 Peter 3:18

We are encouraged to grow in grace. It is only through grace working on the inside that we can deal with our inner desires. It gives you the freedom you seek to walk down a confectionary aisle and not put everything in the trolley.

Through growth in grace you have the discipline to stand before temptation and not give into it.

But as you excel in everything—in faith, in speech, in knowledge, in all earnestness, and in our love for you—see that you excel in this act of grace also.

2 Corinthians 8:7

Push forward in grace and grow in grace and the acts of grace as you would aim to grow in knowledge and love through the Word.

Do not be led away by diverse and strange teachings, for it is good for the heart to be strengthened by grace, not by foods, which have not benefited those devoted to them.

Hebrews 13:9

The comfort of food when in distress, boredom or pleasure is never good to strengthen the heart. Turn to grace, draw near to God.

For the law was given through Moses; grace and truth came through Jesus Christ.

John 1:17

This grace comes through Jesus Christ alone.

And God is able to make all grace abound to you, so that having all sufficiency in all things at all times, you may abound in every good work.

2Corinthians 9:8

This grace is ever ready, and ever present to help you accomplish your goal and good work in all cases

For the grace of God has appeared, bringing salvation for all people, training us to renounce ungodliness and worldly passions, and to live self-controlled, upright, and godly lives in the present age,

Titus 2:11-12

Grace helps you to overcome worldly passions and to live self-controlled. With grace working on the inside, it helps to deal with those things you have being trying to deal with on your own.

Grace is so much more than a covering for sin, it is an enablement for life to help and guide you through situations. You can do much more than you know if you only tap into it.

So I say, walk by the Spirit and you will not gratify the desires of the flesh.

Galatians 5:16

Food for Thought

Chapter 7: Walking in Freedom by the Word

As a teacher, I love sharing the Word of God in everything I do. I feel it helps people to grow and learn more of God.

The Word of God is very strengthening, and you find when you pray it, you get better results and have a stronger prayer life.

It is for that reason that the prayer I have put together for a better relationship with food and better physical health, is loaded with God's Word and his promises over your life.

The Word of God will never return to him void but it will carry out what it was sent to do, Pray the Word and send it back to the Father so it returns to Him with power in your prayers

Prayer for grace, wellbeing and good health

Dear heavenly Father I thank you for your Word in Philippians 4:13 which tells me that "I can do all things through you who strengthens me" You have empowered me with what it takes to succeed in life.

Matthew 19:25 reminds me that "what is impossible with man is possible with God." I know by this that I do not start this journey alone as you are with me.

I thank you for your Word of discipline over my life which encourages me to keep going as there is great reward for me when I do, I stand on the encouragement of Hebrews

12: For the moment all discipline seems painful rather than pleasant, but later it yields the peaceful fruit

Lord I want the springing up of peaceful fruit in my eating and in my health, both in my Soul and Spirit.

I ask you Lord to help me turn over my plate from time to time so I may fast and open myself up more to hearing from heaven and receiving breakthroughs in my life. I want your leading in my life as I stand on Job 23:12 to treasure you word more than my necessary food.

Father I will no longer separate my eating just to the flesh and hold to the knowledge that whatever I do including eating and drinking I do this to bring glory to you according to your Word in 1 Corinthians 10:31

Proverbs 3:5 tells me to trust you more Lord and not lean on my understanding. Father I heed the words in Roman 14:20 not to let food destroy the work of God taking place in my life or the power of fasting I am to get. I ask for understanding so I do not cause anyone else to stumble.

I pray the Holy Spirit will grow His fruit in my life which gives me the power of self-control promised in Galatian 5:22 to help me in those times I am weak.

Father I understand that all things are lawful but not everything I eat is helpful to my body and Spirit. I will not allow food to enslave me according to your word in 1 Corinthians 6:12 & 19 for my body is yours oh Lord and the

Temple of the Holy Spirit. I am not my own I have been bought with a price I belong to you Father.

Lord Jesus, be with me should I become tempted, you tell me in your word 1 Corinthians 10:13 that no temptation will overtake me that is not common to man. You oh God are faithful, and you will not let me be tempted beyond my ability to resist for with the temptation you will also give the way of escape, that I may endure it

Thank you Father for 3 John 1:2 that your desire for me is to be well and in good health as my soul is well, and for your encouraging promise in Isaiah 41:13 reminding me that you are holding my hand and that you are the one who helps me – I do not do this on my own, I do not face these changes for the better on my own.

Dear Lord you do not force my hand, you have put before me Deuteronomy 30:19 to choose, life or death, blessings or curses. I choose life, I choose blessings.

Today with your guiding hands I walk in the Spirit so I will not gratify the desires of my flesh.

Amen.

Notes

Use this page to make note about your personal journey,

- **My Walls to come down**

List area you want to change in your eating

- **My plan for freedom**

List thing you can do to make the changes in your eating

- **My Testimony**

List victories as they come, small or great. Victory is victory

References

The References under Chapter 4 can be found from the following
  sources

New York Times. Article "Fasting Diets Are Gaining Acceptance"

http://well.blogs.nytimes.com/2016/03/07/intermittent-fasting-diets-are-gaining-acceptance/?_r=0

New York Times. Article "95% Regain weight loss"

http://www.nytimes.com/1999/05/25/health/95-regain-lost-weight-or-do-they.html?pagewanted=all

USC University. Article "Fasting triggers stem cell regeneration of
damaged, old immune system"

https://news.usc.edu/63669/fasting-triggers-stem-cell-regeneration-of-damaged-old-immune-system/

The Daily telegraph. Article "Fasting for three days can regenerate
entire immune system, study finds"

http://www.telegraph.co.uk/science/2016/03/12/fasting-for-three-days-can-regenerate-entire-immune-system-study/

The Daily Telegraph. Article "Five day 'fasting' diet slows down
ageing and may add years to life"

http://www.telegraph.co.uk/news/science/science-news/11683736/Five-day-fasting-diet-slows-down-ageing-and-may-add-years-to-life.html

www.ingramcontent.com/pod-product-compliance
Lightning Source LLC
Chambersburg PA
CBHW060143050426
42448CB00010B/2266